I0164295

Orgasmic

Moments

Nah El Publications

Soul Rhymer Productions

Published by Nah El Publications
1255 Race Track Road
Sumter, S.C. 29153

Cover design by Neterankhhotep-El for Soul Rhymer
Productions

Dedication

To all my poets and lovers of erotic word play. Let each poem contained within be whispered, creating eargasms.

Table of Contents

All She Needs

All she need is a kiss from me
As soon as she walks thru the door,
All she need is a good body massage
And to rub her feet when it's sore.
All she need is for me to say
Baby don't worry about dinner,
We can go out to eat or I can eat you out
Either way it's a winner!
All she need is a shoulder to lean on
During the times she's weak,
A kiss on the forehead, a kiss on the eyes,
A kiss on the lips and cheeks.
All she need is for someone to listen
And understand her pain,
All she need is for the sun to shine
And dry up all the rain.
All she need is for tears to stop
So she can clearly see,
She don't have to be bound in chains
anymore

Because I have the key.
To set her free and spread her wings
And fly toward the heavens,
All she need is for someone to appreciate
her presence and her essence.

By My Side

Come and lay by my side
There's nothing more to do,
Than to stare into each other eyes
And behold the beauty of two.
Two loving souls so kind
And gentle with the other,
But the force when it's combined
Creates a father and mother.

The Sun and Moon
(Under the Stars)

A hot summer's night
We lay down, looking up,
Captivated by the lights
So far away from the touch.
Darkness surrounds us
But fear is not a factor,
The silence is loud but
We're alone in the pasture.
Like cattle grazing, we are gazing
Off into the distance,
Of time and space amazed with
Our emotions in this instance.
You rest your head on my chest
Singing sweet melodies,
This is bliss I must confess
It feels so heavenly.
Your voice soothes my weary heart
My hand eases your tension,

You and I playing our part
On Earth, in this dimension.
The moon beneath the moon
The sun beneath the stars,
The sun and moon, yet in tuned
Fireflies in the jars.
Illumination within the glass
A cool light breeze seems to pass,
The smell of night, the smell of grass
The silence broken by a laugh.
I squeeze your body tight
Till our bodies begin to merge,
It feels just right, it feels like
The sensation of a power surge.
This should be life, husband and wife
Looking at stars above,
Till morning come and back to night
Such a small world with boundless love.

The symbol for OM or AUM.

A Hindu sacred sound used in mantras. The sound that created the Universe.
Some believe the Universe was created from a big bang. Perhaps it was an Orgasmic Moment. (OM)

Thunder Storm 1

For once the weatherman is right
Smells like rain is in the air,
I can feel the change in the temperature
While I'm playing in your hair.
While standing on the steps
it begins to drizzle,
I pull you close and palm your ass
As you laugh and giggle.
Let's go inside are the words you whispered
Let's stay outside is what I suggested,
Now up against the wall and spread them,
Just like you're getting arrested.
A little rain won't hurt, as a matter of fact
The wetter it is the better,
Meow, meow, your pussy's all wet
I hope you don't mind me petting her.
Overhead is a dark cloud, oops my bad,
It's just your pussy in my face,
They say be careful what you wish for
Hell, I guess I did ask for a taste.

Rain on me, rain on me, sweet rain water
Sweet till the last drop,
Oh how I love these thunderstorms
And wish they never stop.
Before she left, damn, damn, damn,
She really blew my mind,
I watched her throw her pussy in the air
Then it came down as sunshine!

Thunder Storm 2

It's raining once again
Listen to it as it hits the roof,
You're dealing with a magician and yes
I can make your bra and panties go-"poof!"
I love when it pours continuously
Hell... I'm hoping that it floods,
I just hope we don't get carpet burns
From rolling on this rug.
All the pounding that I'm doing
Shaking the whole house like some thunder,
Hot, steamy, and sweaty love we make
Got it feeling like it's summer.
Multiple orgasms that we share
Got me roaring like a lion,
You're shaking trying to catch your breath
Feeling like you're dying.
The storm has yet to pass
And lightning continues to flash,
We're both on cloud nine it seems
Hoping the plane don't crash.

Electrical charges throughout your body
Pulsations that you emit,
The sensations you can't describe
The temptations you can't resist.
Each kiss I place along your spine
Produces an aftershock,
Your body has become extremely sensitive
You whisper, damn don't stop.

Lotus Flower

The lotus flower grows and rises from a murky pond and yet beautiful petals bloom. They symbolize purity and rebirth. A red lotus is a symbol of love and passion.

What is SEX???

What is SEX???

What is SEX???

What is SEX???

What is SEX???

What is SEX???

What is SEX???

What is SEX???

What is SEX???

What is SEX???

What is SEX???

What is SEX???

What is SEX???

What is SEX???

What is SEX???

What is SEX???

Lips

Her thick lips cast a spell with ease
I'm compelled by her energy,
Her kisses are worth dying for
But her kisses breathe life in me.
Sweet nectar from a Goddess
Like a child suckling his mother,
The sustenance that nourishes my soul
Cannot be provided by another.
When I taste her lips, stars explode
The seas expand and the land erodes,
My heart it spins all out of control
Desire consumes me and takes a hold.
See, her lips are amazing!
I love her lips!
I pull her close.
I grip her hips.
Our souls they merge
When I take a sip,
I kiss her over and over
And over and over and over, yeah.

Probably my favorite part of her body
Her eyes come in second,
I bet if I stared into her eyes
And kissed her lips, I'd cum in seconds.
Her presence I desire often
Often the fire rages within,
Only her cool lips can soothe me so
Never do I have to pretend.
Like I'm feeling her just a little
These hands feeling her just a lot,
As I'm feeling her on her booty
And as I'm feeling her on that spot.
What I'm feeling is what I'm feeling
And I know she's feeling hot,
Just say what you're feeling baby
Say whatever but just not stop.
Your lips on my lips
My lips on your lips,
I'm talking one, two, three
Yeah, all four lips.
I love your lips.
They drive me crazy.

Attraction

I'm attracted to you physically
You fit perfect inside my arms,
You're the missing piece to my puzzle
You need a king and not a pawn.
I be up from dusk to dawn
From dawn to dusk again,
It'll crush what's left of my heart
If to me, you are just a friend.
See, I can no longer just pretend
What I'm feeling is something light,
What I'm feeling is something right
See, I'm feeling it with all my might.
I'm attracted to you mentally
Your strong mind blows mine,
I'm hanging on every thought you speak
Like a t-shirt on a clothes line.
Intelligence is the new sexy
Stimulate me with your wisdom,
Make my brain work up a sweat
As it dances to your sacred rhythm.

The Root Chakra symbol

The human body is composed of 7 major
chakras (energy vortexes).
The root chakra is located at the base of
your spine and deals with survival, instincts
and sexual energy or potentiality from the
lower self.

These Naughty Thoughts of Mine

How can I not fall for such beauty?
Heaven knows you're easy on the eyes,
These same eyes which undress you
And visualize squeezing your thighs.
Pardon these naughty thoughts of mine
Especially when you belong to a King,
I wish not to come between a Royal family
With some wild erotic fling.

Our Secret

If I grabbed you by your arms
Or either your waist,
Would you tremble with fear?
Tell me if your body would shake.
If I squeezed your body tight
And get all in your face,
Tell me, would it be
An uncomfortable place?
If I looked you in the eyes
And gave you a kiss,
Would you go back home
And tell your man all this?
Would you push me or slap me?
Even if you liked it?
Would you give into temptation
Or continue to fight it?
What if you loved it?
And the way that you felt,
Couldn't be described with words except...
Made your body melt.

When you're home in your bed
Do you touch yourself?
Does it flow like an ocean?
Do you rub your breast?
When you're with him
Do you think of me?
Can you read my thoughts
And feel my energy?
Dam it!!! You know we have chemistry!

My Feelings

I shouldn't feel the way I do
But I can't control my heart,
All day thinking of you
Is my foremost thoughts.
The way your body feels
When pressed against mine,
Our souls begin to merge
And become intertwined.
The state of peace and happiness
Whenever you are near,
Truly I know that I am blessed
My life, my love, my dear.

Stir It Like Coffee

When I look into your eyes
It makes my nature rise,
It's only natural and I
Can't control myself.
See, I hold myself, I told myself
If I hold her breasts,
Then behold, what's next?
We're on the floor with sex.
Carpet burns as we turn
Like the world do,
Work hard, play hard and grind hard
As I stir you.
Stir it like coffee.
Stir it like coffee.
The sex is hot.
Better proceed with caution.

Min

A predynastic neter of Kemet (Egypt).
A neter of fertility and sexuality. Easily
recognized by an erect phallus and a raised
arm holding a flail.

What is PASSION???

What is PASSION???

What is PASSION???

What is PASSION???

What is PASSION???

What is PASSION???

What is PASSION???

What is PASSION???

What is PASSION???

What is PASSION???

What is PASSION???

What is PASSION???

What is PASSION???

What is PASSION???

What is PASSION???

What is PASSION???

Polishing My Royal Scepter

She led me to the bedroom
And there she undressed me,
She was fully clothed still
Looking so sexy.
Taking charge like a lady
Demanding me to relax,
She pushed me onto the bed
And then climbed in to my lap.
Forced my head back on the pillow
As she went for my neck,
Left her mark on the right side
Then went for my chest.
Licking and biting me
Her aim was to please,
Kissing my abs
This is more than a tease.
Head bowed like in prayer
She reached for my rod,
Engulfing the tip

She started to slob.
I'm clutching my fists
My toes even curl,
She gave it a lick
And proceeded to swirl.
Fighting the urge
But I'm losing control,
Telling her stop
But she swallows my soul.
Sensitivity's heighten
I blacked out for a second,
Am I coming or going?
I needed directions.
Looking down at my scepter
It was shining like gold,
Still feeling rich
Although I relinquished a load.

Sometimes

Sometimes, it's not love at first sight
Sometimes, it's love over time,
Sometimes, I'm in love with your body
Sometimes, I'm in love with your mind.
Sometimes, your words are so bitter
Sometimes, your kisses are so sweet,
Sometimes, you appear to be strong
Sometimes, you appear to be weak.
Sometimes, I'm loving your absence
Sometimes, I'm hating your presence,
Sometimes, I'm missing you baby
Sometimes, I need your essence.
Sometimes, there's joy in my heart
Sometimes, the frustration runs wild,
Sometimes, I see an adult
Sometimes, I see a small child.
Sometimes, I cringe at your touch
Sometimes, I love how it feels,
Sometimes, it's too good to be true
Sometimes, I know it's not real.

What Would You Do

What would you do
If I grabbed you by the wrist,
And pull your body close to mine
And gave you a kiss?
I mean, what would you do
If all the doors were closed,
And I couldn't control myself
And ripped off all your clothes?
For real for real, what would you do
If I threw you on the bed,
And while your heart beating all fast
I said, throw up your legs?
Seriously, what would you do
If I kissed your heavenly gates,
And lick and suck and lick and suck
Until your body shakes?
And then what would you do
If I slowly, slowly entered,
And stirred it like coffee
All so gentle?

Tell me, what would you do
If I picked you up in the air,
With your legs wrapped around my waist
And just hold you there?
Ok then, what would you do
After an hour pass on the clock,
And I slapped you on your bottom
And said, hop on top?
Hypothetically speaking, what would you do
If I was into some tantra,
Would you be ready and willing
To say my name like a mantra?

Serpent

The serpent is widely known to symbolize
fertility, immortality and sex. Kundalini or
the sexual energy residing in the root chakra
is said to resemble a coiled serpent. The Hopi
people of North America performed a snake
dance which celebrated the union between
the sky and underworld spirits which
renewed the fertility of nature. In the Bible

it is the serpent which introduced sexuality to Adam and Eve as their eyes were opened and they were able to see their nakedness after eating the forbidden fruit.

Kitchen

I see your heart
I know it's pure,
I may be hesitant
But I know you're sure.
Your hand is out
For me to lead,
Your soil is fertile
In need of seeds.
I give you knowledge
I reap your wisdom,
A nurturing spirit
That reaches children.
Tears you shed
When your heart is heavy,
Emotions flow
Like a broken levee.
Your eyes they speak
As my heart listens,
A starving soul
And I'm a kitchen.

Picturing Peaceful Moments with You

Too often you're in my head
So, I visualize you in my bed,
Resting from last night escapade
As I'm rubbing on your legs.
Staring at your pretty face
Sleeping sound, knowing you're safe,
Since good things come to those who wait
I know I deserve great.
I deserve a taste of your cakes
Your pies and whatever else you bake,
I don't believe in fate
The time and proper place is what I create.
You move slightly but still sleep
Something about you so sweet,
Running my fingers across your cheeks
I could just lay here for weeks.
No makeup and still you glow
When you wake up will you still go?

Or will you stay as our love grow?
  Our energies they still flow.

Ankh

The Kemetic (Egyptian) symbol for life. It is also said that the upper loop portion of the ankh represents the womb of woman and the lower portion represents the phallus of man.

What is LOVE???

What is LOVE???

What is LOVE???

What is LOVE???

What is LOVE???

What is LOVE???

What is LOVE???

What is LOVE???

What is LOVE???

What is LOVE???

What is LOVE???

What is LOVE???

What is LOVE???

What is LOVE???

What is LOVE???

What is LOVE???

Before You Go

Before you walk away
Before you close that door,
Bring that ass back to me baby
Let's do it just once more.
Let's take it nice and slow
Kiss me here, I'll lick you there,
Bite me here, I'll kiss you there
I'll bite you too, to keep it fair.
I love it when you moan
I love it when you shake,
I love going down on you
I love the way you taste.

Picture It

Picture us making love
Even if we started from lust,
Even if we started from scratch
You scratching my back till I bust.
I'm going in deep as you cuss
Your good loving, I can't get enough,
Let me rewind the frame for you
Why don't you say my name for me?
This isn't a game baby
This is insane, crazy.
Crazy how bad I want to taste you,
Crazy how bad I want to embrace you.
Licking your body from toe to head
Started on the floor to bed,
From the bed to the couch
We both have wobbly legs.

The Older The Berry
(The Sweeter the Juice)

Cougar... cougar... who? Her!

Look, I'm going to be straight up and down
Cause that's the only way I know how to be,
My question to you is, can you see
Yourself spending the night with me?
Now I don't want to hear none of that
Boy I'm old enough to be your momma,
Well if it makes you happy you can
Call me son after I slide out your punana.
Now I notice you noticing me
Noticing you,
And even though it's a short notice
We can still do what we do.
Now I'm a man of action
And my action last till sun up,
But if you want to talk, fine, sit on my lap
We'll talk about the first thing that cums up.

Can you dig it?

With one kiss, I bet I'll have your panties
So wet you'll have to ring them out,
Anticipating the shaft and the tip
Yelling, bring 'em out, bring 'em out.
It's hard to yell
With pillows in your mouth,
Bring 'em out, bring 'em out,
It's hard to yell
With my gun up in your mouth.
But really, age aint nothing
But a number like 69,
And things get better with age
Like bottled wine.
Or so I was told, I need confirmation
So anxious to sip from your cup,
And you can bet your ass and half a titty
For at least three nuts.

He and She

He wants to be with she
As she lays on the chest of he,
Listening to the heartbeats of he
He holds the hand of she.
And with the other hand of he
Touching the face that belongs to she,
No words being exchanged.
No music is playing.
As he and she are being still in the moment,
There's a dance of chemistry.
He's feeling the energy
For she's a beautiful entity,
He's really into she
Hoping for true intimacy.
The life of he, many years passed
To discover a love which heals that,
Empty space that often feels bad
But the love of she conceals cracks.
She kisses the lips of he
Biting the fruits of the forbidden tree,

Now opened are the eyes of she
Seeing God, she acknowledges he.
She yearns to build a dynasty
So much knowledge she gains from he,
So much wisdom displayed by she
They overstand it's we.

The Akkadian/Sumerian
Goddess Ishtar

Goddess of fertility and war. Ishtar went to
the underworld and there she was impaled
and hung. Days later she rose from the
underworld. Ishtar is where the word Easter
comes from.

Sex, Love and More Sex
(Sip somethin')

Baby come here
I said, Bring that ass here!
Let me make this clear.
We're going to start with this glass here.
(Sip somethin')
I want you to get loose
Feel the vibes I produce,
Let your hair down
And kick off your shoes.
Let your dress fall to the floor
Like Autumn leaves,
I want you to breathe with ease
Relax, relate, release…
Your titteez from your bra
And Ahhh…
Drop them draws.
(And sip somethin')
See, I'm trying to ease the tension
In your neck and lower back,

So, I keep a bottle of body oil
Over where the sofa's at.
(Lay down)
A full body massage
Is on the agenda,
So, when I'm rubbing you down
It's like I'm preparing my dinner.
Don't worry
I won't bite,
Unless that's something
You like.
Like...bite marks on your ass cheeks
And inner thighs,
Like your nipples protruding
As your temperature rise.
(I need to sip somethin')
I'm trying to touch something
Rub something,
Kiss something
Lick something.
I want your pelvic region to feel
As if multiple explosions are taking place,
I want you biting your lips
As you cover your face.

(Your momma???
She can't help you right now)
You're about to enter the course
Where souls intertwine and merge with the source.
Oh God! Oh God!
(God is in you)
I don't think you heard me.
I said, God is... in... you.
Let that marinate,
Let your hips gyrate.
(I need a sip. You need a sip? Sip somethin')
Feel as our heartbeats
Become synced,
Two bodies, one heart, one mind
We're linked.
There's no time but now
The moment's forever,
This is love, this is sex,
This is you getting wetter.
(Sip somethin')

Shiva Lingam

In Hinduism, a symbol of the god Shiva and the goddess Shakti. The shaft is representative of man and centered in a disk-shaped object, representing the yoni of woman.

What is POETRY???
What is POETRY???
What is POETRY???
What is POETRY???
What is POETRY???
What is POETRY???
What is POETRY???
What is POETRY???
What is POETRY???
What is POETRY???
What is POETRY???
What is POETRY???
What is POETRY???
What is POETRY???
What is POETRY???
What is POETRY???

How Edible Are You

How edible are you?
As I fix my eyes on your milk chocolate skin,
I wish to indulge in your temptations of sin.
To taste the caramel pleasures within
Your sweet juices are like an explosion
In my orals, causing me to grin.
(I... have a sweet tooth for you baby.)
Lately I found myself daydreaming
Of licking you from your toes to your head,
And my night dreams
Aren't too easy on my bed.

Waking up in a sticky situation.
Fascinated by your buns.

My tongue...cries out
Can I be your wash rag?
Can I be your towel?
It's a guarantee that I'll have you speaking in
tongues or confusing your speech like the

tower of Babel.
I'm just babbling.
But how edible are you?
It's mind raveling.
My mind's traveling
Thoughts of kissing you, licking you,
Sucking you, biting you...
But lightly.
Aren't you a delightful bite
As I stuff my face?
Your cream on my lips, I lick it off
I always wanted to get a taste...
Of heaven.
My palates in a frenzy
How edible are you?
Put you on a plate with biscuits and gravy
and (Sluuurrrrrrrp) Sop you up.
Hours later as my tongue
clings to my roof,
I want to say I have this taste in my mouth
Oh yeah, it's you.
Walking around looking like I ate a
Box of glazed doughnuts.
How edible are you?

Skilled in the lethal art of tongue-fu.
(What you know about that?)
My tongue could sure use some exercise.
How edible are you?
How flexible are you?
How flexible are your hours?
What are you doing right now?
How edible are you?

Caught Up

I'm caught up between loving you
Liking you and lusting you,
I'm not sure which one it is
But since we're discussing you...
I'm just curious to know
Is there someone cuffing you?
Touching you? Hugging you?
Trusting you?
I hate to make an ass out of myself
By assuming but I assume so,
Ask me why? Because look at yourself
You're so beautiful.
Tongue tied when you're near so I'll stay
On the other side of the room door,
You hardly even notice me, so why am I
thinking about jumping the broom for?
Or thinking about jumping the moon for?
You're the only one I swoon for,
Sure as heaven if I could sing

You'll be the only one I croon for.
Play a tune for, heart beating like
The drum of a shaman entering a trance,
Let's dance, let's take a chance
Let's — camp!
Out somewhere while laying on our backs
While gazing at stars,
Anxious about kissing you under the
Moonlight got my heart racing like cars.
Hold my hand, feel the nervous twitch
Every now and again,
Honeysuckles smell sweet
But not as sweet as your skin.
Come a little closer
Until our auras merge,
Electricity's in the air
I can feel every surge.

Sex Talk

My lips on your lips
My chest on your breasts,
That's a heart to heart
Communication during sex.
You screaming my name
I whisper in your ear
Come on and cum
I know that orgasm is near.
Climax for me once
Climax for me twice,
All that noise that you were talking
Now you're paying the price.
Calling for God
Like I don't show you a sign,
I may not cum when you need me
But I'm always on time.
You saying it's mine
And I'm saying I know,
It's supposed to be a quickie
But I'm taking it slow.

Hush, let me do what I do.

Timeless

I'm feeling her energy
A beautiful entity,
I'm hoping she's into me
I can show her true intimacy.
Stimulating her senses
Removing her walls and her fences,
At ease but she tenses
From stomach kisses she clinches.
Pillows and bed sheets
I'm making her legs weak,
Carrying these feelings till next week
This is after the sex peaks.
The love that her heart feels
I'm playing the part real,
Nothing's fake when the dark seals
Our fate spinning like cartwheels.
The union between souls
Intersecting like crossroads,
The tingling in ten toes
Lasting forever like time froze.

Tantric Sex is a high form of sex.

Tantric, from the word tantra means to woven as in the physical and spiritual bodies of the practitioners and humanity with God. In tantric sex, extended orgasms are achieved minus ejaculation. Energy is depleted from the body during ejaculation and the aim is to preserve and build energy during tantric sex.

Other Books by the Author

1. Nia & Khalid What Rhymes With...???
2. Nia & Khalid Bye Bye Cry Baby
3. Boys Don't Keep Dairies (Malik's Journal)
4. AllRite, My Sun
5. Black Women Crying Out for Love and Help
6. Appetite for Destruction
7. Unspoken Words, Beautifully Written
8. A Chaotic Love

Connect with the Author

Neterankhhotep-el@hotmail.com

www.neterankhhotep-el.com

www.facebook.com/neterankhhotep

OM

OM

OM

OM

OM

OM

OM

OM

OM

OM

OM

OM

OM

OM

OM

www.ingramcontent.com/pod-product-compliance
Lightning Source LLC
Chambersburg PA
CBHW060714030426
42337CB00017B/2860